Something *Hungry* Just Woke Up

Something *Hungry* Just Woke Up

poems

AMANDA DZIMIANSKI

The characters and events in this book are fictitious. Any resemblance to real persons, living or dead, is coincidental.

Copyright © 2025 Amanda Dzimianski

All rights reserved. No parts of this book may be reproduced in any form or by any electronic or mechanical means, including information storage and retrieval systems, without the express written permission of the author, except for the use of brief quotations in reviews.

ISBN: 979-8-9869411-2-7 (paperback)

Cover design: Copyright © 2025 Amanda Dzimianski
Cover photo: Copyright © Dirk "Beeki" Schumacher via Canva.com
Back cover photo: Copyright © Alejandro Correa Bayardo via Unsplash.com

Author website: amandadzimianski.com

First Printing, 2025

for the famished parts

Table of Contents

Author's note

Mother Wound of the Wolf Daughter	1
Cognitive Revolution	2
Good Leather	4
Book of Judges	5
I've Pulled One Too Many Cards	7
When the Sun Goes Down in Winter	8
Mosaic	10
Scull Shoals	13
The Spiritual Discipline of Alchemical Writing	17
Imagine if Jephthah's daughter…	18
Hitman	23
Monster	24
Poetics	29
Split	31
Ten Word Poems	
Doomed Romance	
Favorite Compliment from Therapy	
My Mom Would Say…	35
body diptych	36
What Dreamers Do	38

[ ]	41
The Trade	43
Strawberry Fields	47
Guardian	48
My friend says a sea anemone closes up when touched	49
Curon	54
i thought it'd feel different	56
The Thing with Fangs	61
Venus Retrograde	62
h/ex	65
Canyon	66
Bottom of the Wheel	68
Strange, Small Town	72
seventeen	73
Not Cold Anymore	76
The Tender Untethered	78

Notes	*81*
Content Advisement	*83*
Acknowledgments	*85*

Author's Note

A confession: the deepest wounds in my life have not come through what was spoken, but by what never was. Sometimes by others, sometimes by myself.

I'm learning that to speak a hard thing is to offer options, to open up pathways of choice that didn't exist before — a practice that helps to architect a culture of consent, through all layers of life.

And, consent must be mutual. In that spirit of both speaking hard things and offering space for choice, please know that these pages contain themes of religious trauma and abuse, sexual assault, and mental health struggles. For those it can serve, you will find detailed content advisement on page 83.

Know that if you find certain poems too emotionally heavy of a lift some days, you have not 'failed' as a reader; you have simply exercised a kind of autonomy for yourself. Listen to your why.

If you breeze right through, and wonder what the fuck I'm talking about (my content warnings do not cover swearing, sorry), you have not 'failed' as a reader; you have simply identified a kind of autonomy for yourself. Listen to your how.

~

I'm honored that you're reading this — thank you. I invite you to heed your hunger. I believe all expression of lack is an honest experience of need, regardless of how we choose to fill the empty spaces. Your desire to be nourished, love, will always hand you the keys to yourself. May you set yourself free.

— Amanda

August, 2025

Mother Wound of the Wolf Daughter

what do you do
when you belong to a mother
whose foot is caught
in a trap

      merciless ripshard teeth
      fresh red staining limb
      bone glinting in the moonlight

and She swears
that this
is freedom?

      you can taste fear
      rippling from her chest

      you watch the snowfields
      of her eyes bloom

She says
the wilderness is the snare
and the danger is named
hunger

She says
daughter
put your foot here in the steel
with me

Cognitive Revolution

I slash the lettuce in the kitchen
Slubbed and ripply green
Under my fingertips

He walks in
In one breath reveals the backstitching
There were other kinds of humans
While my mind scrapes
                         shifts
                             shuttles
Through all the possibilities
My body already knows the truth of it

Splitting leaf from spine
I still ask
         What happened to them?

Reluctant fact unfurls
We killed them
Our kind
How does the same sound
        'kind'
Ferry both meanings?

Vegetable viscera stains the cutting board
Viridescent corpses
Spread out across the surface

I want to believe
Eradication was an unattached cruelty
Ice and famine
Nature's own knife
My body knows the knotted truth of it

While the world has warped and yet keeps weaving
Ancient synapses snap across etheric threads
I stand at this machinated countertop
   a microdot
I know in needles
They were here
   and now they're gone
   and I am here
      and will be gone

He turns on the faucet and I
Watch the water drain
   down, down
     below
I ache to turn it off
And do not move

Life looms without pause
I have been shot into
   something
Holding skeins across the time frame
A clueless weaver

Good Leather

My hope used to be shiny,
bright. Fresh, like the first snow.

I discovered, like winter's whitewash,
time   changes things.

Pristine fleece swiftly grays. There is slick,
slurping mud lurking beneath. Invisible ice.

Endless cycles of frostbite, with this
as the constant: a destiny of melting.

So I've traded in my ghostish powder for good
leather. Something hand-stitched, salt-stained,

and historied. Now, instead of the snow,
hope's the boots for walking through it.

Book of Judges

The women's bible study gathered
    clutching styrofoam cups
    in a conference room, third floor of the fancy church
Flimsy pages fluttered in the sunshine
    wings stapled to earth
We breasted the query: "Why did god
    let the Israelite men throw away their wives?"

        Canonical hatred for divorce apparently depends
                on who's serving the papers

Hovering ardent, still stained white, we rallied
    in a desert, orbiting the idol of faithful ignorance
This was the safe answer: to say, "I don't know"
    instead of daring the audacity of certainty
Like swords of smoke, our stabs at answers dissolved
Meek and quiet, we swallowed back the bile of Eve's blame
Bore Hagar's abandonment to a thirstland
Suffered the shameless barter of the bodies of daughters
Sick-stomached the butchery of an unnamed woman's corpse,
    her life raped out of her by a neighborhood mob of men

        That "good book" always tastes so sweet to angry boys

We plucked crumbs from between carpet fibers
    called it a feast
No one could dream
    of myth

    while being forced
    into shapes to fulfill prophecy

        Some knowings unfurl slow, like a silken dawn
                Hunger can be a beautiful thing

Someday, starving and blistered
    we'd stumble back to the beginning
See the seams carefully covered over by wallpaper
Feel forked-lightning rage flash in our veins
    over every betrayal baptized as "purity"
Scent enough sulfur in Eden
Vomit up enough dead wafers in a promised land
Ache our way into becoming our own
    open-eyed judges

Under the sun of our sisters, we'd become match-lit alive
    unfiltered by stained glass
Breathe a stardust still sparking with mystery
Become less virtuous
More ravenous
Savor the honeyed grace of some sky-wide, stringless love
Cagebreak our souls

Then, like Jael
    hell-bent and righteous
    we'd drive a sharpened stake
    through god's head

I've Pulled One Too Many Cards

My final swallow of the fairy tale is darkly sweet & silty.
Will the muse show up if I give birth to rose petals & scatter

them on my altar? *High Priestess crossed.* 'Muse' is just 'use'
with 'm' on the front — 'm' for 'mouth' & 'mine' & 'madness.'

Empress reverse. My resume is unimpressive. *Five of Pentacles.*
The manifestation coach on YouTube says to try a cinnamon candle.

Pearl glint in the window glass reminds me of *The Moon* that night
you let go too quickly. *Two of Cups, straight into the shredder.*

A ripped seam, I wept threads. Does anyone get what they want?
Does anyone tell the truth about what they want? Or about

what it's like to get it? *Nine of Fucking Swords.* Finger-prick on a
spindle & just the right amount of blood is supposed to pacify

the disenchanted. *Fool upright.* I've pulled one too many cards.
This isn't about the story ending; it's about mine becoming more.

When the Sun Goes Down in Winter

I step beyond the threshold
    into stretched-out shadows
        and I'm sorry
            I can't rewind
                to the young light.

I feel the bitter bite of the shade,
    see the slant of the sun
        along the iced roof angle,
            catch it glancing on the curved
                gooseneck of the streetlamp.

There's a crystal crunch under my soles
    and I want caution tape
        stuck across my fragile moments,
            criss-crossing them in some safe
                embrace of satisfaction guaranteed.

Still street becomes glass time capsule,
    collecting all of us
        in a clustered solitude,
            in a tense-present breath-holding,
                lighting candles against the cold.

I tread a tunnel hemmed by clock tick and place,
    the minutes marking the march of a relentless daystar
        warring toward the sill of the sky,
            just to disappear
                and drench us in the dark.

I've read the words
    about the gentle twilight goddess
        kindly enclosing the world in her cloak.
            But I know it's Night that's coming on
            and her coat is heavy.

There's an ache in my chest
    for where I've never been
        and where I've always been.
            I'm frozen in this moment
                finding everything is thin.

Mosaic

They've done an art project in the second-grade classroom

A collage
Composed of tiny, colorful things
All cut into pieces
Radiating outward from a dark, red center

Striking shades are visible:
A noisy orange is 'September fire'
'Lights out' signals a charcoal navy blue
A deep, vibrant crimson, 'rose blood'

'This is about power,' the critic on my left declares
An observer in front insists, 'it's about pain'
The journalist scribbles a headline
'Students display vulnerability, depth of emotion'

The exhibition required demolition
A breaking down of what already existed
Within a fragile whole
Something destroyed in order to make
A statement

This is called 'a right'

The scraps are scatter-shot across the canvas
Cockeyed angles
Unimaginable shapes

Everyone practiced for today

Spectators will later dub this
'A cycle of resilience'

Grief does not care about resilience

The design is sagging
Riddled with holes
I listen to eulogies
Naming beloved fragments
Lost in the rendering

How much is vanishing
In the invention of our stories?
Intention twisted and wrung out empty
Meaning ripped from the root of the tongue

No one who sees
The bodies
Of work
Is ever the same

This was not supposed to be a poem
About guns

Art exists because of need

The art project is a mosaic
Which is always a shattered mirror
Reflecting back every broken truth

My world looks like a pulsing wound

I must

Lean in closer

Scull Shoals

The river is swollen.

Remains of rust brick walls jut from the earth
like broken teeth.
Stone foundations receding,
being swallowed by what's alive.
Wreck and ruin squat here and now
in this leafy gap carved from the forest.

Diamond edges of light cut through the spring's chill.

In the cracks of quiet between our chatter,
I catch the noise of traffic intruding through the trees
over the rush of the wide waters.

I've heard that in the fog, or on a lonely day
in thin-veil seasons,
you can feel
sylphic spirits move among the copses.
Some say this place is haunted, enthralled
by the uneasy dead.

Who does the land belong to?
is always the question, but the wrong one.

Who lives like they belong to the land?
scrapes into something truer.

When we learned about the so-called wars,
I begged you to ask,
*What part of the story
isn't being told?*

I have to believe the land knows
when tender hearts walk her ribs.
I want to believe this.
Then again, fire and flood took the innocent, too.

Love is mythology —
invented meaning we make up to serve as flimsy seacraft
upon oceans of pain.
Chemical ships evolved for survival.
We've labeled adoration our finest achievement,
a bright banner flown fierce,
to distract ourselves
from the imminence of destruction.

This is what I tell myself
to make letting you go
feel safer.

The news says the dire wolves have come back.
Really, they're just regular wolves
spliced with some ancient DNA.

Isn't that what we're always doing?
Trying to recreate the past with our found scraps,
hoping it turns out to be less endangered
this time?

White dudes on a podcast say *scull* is a derivative
spelling of *skull,* and is an attribution to the bodies
unburied by the river.
I hear the echoes of all our losses.

But *scull* is also a kind of oar,
the vessel it steers,
and the movement of both.
Scull means skimming across the stream,
staying on top of the surface.

During childhood swim lessons at the Y, sculling
was my favorite drill —
lying back, being supported
by the depth of an entire pool, feet fluttering,
hands and arms making rhythmic pulses of motion
to propel my body onward.

The world was muted, everything buoyant,
and the ceiling was far, far above.
I didn't think about anyone dying,
even while drowning
was just one
wrong breath away.

Trekking through the tall grass, we find
a turtle shell rotting hollow, large
as a human head.
I wonder what pulled it so far from home.

I wonder whether what killed it
was the leaving,
or the trying to return.

It's springtime.
I ignore the roiled sepia of the tributary,
the text from a friend about the quad of eggs
vanished without a trace
from the cardinal's nest by her window.

I feel the dark around us,
but I cannot see it
against the brightness dazzling my eyes.

Scull means not drowning
this time.

We splash our blanket in the deep green
and are held.

The Spiritual Discipline of Alchemical Writing
A Golden Shovel after Wendell Berry

Shivering slow, these
are the final, rattling passings
of a cultivated peace. I've bled to resurrect
all we've lost. Senescence begs a
blank page, something less than joy
, a wish to unspin what is. Without
ink in my spine, barren ground becomes defect
running too deep to defeat, the
scar scarlet-lettering life
, a crop-shorn account that
confines. But this juddering pen steps
beyond every borderland and
the tuning voice of Time's river sings
stubborn in the dark. In
the spiral of current, walls become ways
. I have written open the stolen field of
myself — proof every seed's alive through death.

Imagine if Jephthah's daughter doesn't have a name because she was a witch and they just wanted to erase her
for the daughters

You wrote me
wrong. You said I went willingly.
Submissive. Cooperative.
Consensually participating.

Conveniently,
every chronicle of your sacrifices
goes this way.
Jesus. Isaac. "Some war hero's daughter."

We were the steel spine of your book.
We held the whole story
together.

You didn't even afford me
the dignity of a name.

This was my sin:
I loved you, and ran to you.
You blamed me.

Through the smoke
rings
I vowed to haunt you.

Eve has grown a fur coat.
She howls
My Name
every full moon outside the garden.
The angels with their burning swords
tremble.

                                        Voice of one
                                    you abandoned
                                  in the wilderness:

Time is a cold, old tick
-et to someplace everybody's already been.
Familiarity breeds contemp
-latives and devotees to splinters.
Repetition, repetition! Grooves sworn in
-to the roots and flesh,
spinning lack into your genes
-is of doubt.

Stakes and crosses are cut from the same
shame-sown forest.

I have flown to and fro
walking up and down.
I did not find the devil you spoke of.
I found only little godlings.

See, the testament tattooed along my ribs:
"In the beginning"

fear
created the heavens and the hells.

Men said "let us put lies
into the mouths of gods
and call it light."

"Subdue the earth"
  meant
conquer the mother
  which is to say
keep the Love in chains.

All my magic was too much for you.
It always is.

Unwilling to sit within the peace of mystery,
unarmored,
you chose the weakest form of power.

Atone me this:
biblical law states
that if a woman doesn't scream for help
while being raped
she should be stoned alongside her rapist.

In the dick-swinging contests between gods
the daughters
are always
the deep-throated tale
you refuse to tell.

I am sick of redeeming your stories.

You
You cannot buy
You cannot buy back blood.

Scorched souls and cinders
are the works of your hands!
Grace is forever
a one-way street and this weeping camel
has gouged out
the eye of your needle.

I summoned the coven
-ant of the sisters across space
and wheelspin. The divin
-ation showed me men's minds
still en caul
-droned in immortality.

You have no ears to hear.

I, Daughter With No Name,
stand here at your crossroads.
I smell the smoke of flaming altars.

You call me "Heretic."
Come seize me, then.
Which one of us
will burn tonight?
Come and see.

Bring your files for my fangs —
I will sharpen them into razors.

Bring your straw for the stake —
I will twist it into whips.

Your white flag? Sheared into ribbons
to wrap as garters around my naked thighs.

>Thus saith the Women you have silenced:
*I am no weapon
in your unholy wars.
I will be no burnt offering.*

*Choose you this day
whom you will serve, whether the fathers
who made god in their own image
to seize dominion over your spirits,
or the fathers who turned their faces away
in the stone-cold hours of injustice.*

*As for me and my teeth,
we will serve an honest lore.*

*As for me and my red tent?
We will serve cunt.*

Hitman

On West 46th Street
I watch the shadows
shift
around you.
I don't think you
even know they're there,
though you called your demons
by their first names.

In Time's Square
the sparkle is glare
on your skin.
The sheen turns you ghost-like.
I joke that this isn't the right time
for hiding and hazy cloaks.
You grin, ask
But what about daggers?

While the stab wound
weeps
predictably
you've disappeared.

Monster

It's a January dusk.
Amidst winter's bitterswell of beauty
the monster has come awake.
(By this I mean I, myself.)
Befriend it, they've all said.
They aren't wrong,
but she doesn't want friends.
She wants freedom,
from this cage, from the bars
we've been bloodying my fists against.

I drive away, shaking my damn head at how I make
theater out of every distress. Just like a god.

The old road is impossibly flat and straight,
relic of an era I don't remember.
It's wide and long and dry.
I floor the gas
until self-preservation
baptizes my anger in fear.
(As if they are different.)

Passing church after church,
their pointed roofs pretending to reach somewhere,
I turn left at the light, buzz against the wrinkled
margins of my spiraling lane. I keep watch
for the turnoff to a place I've been before.
It isn't exactly a church, kind of is.

Has a view of still waters, green pastures.
I went last time in a different, more interesting crisis.
I got quiet. I heard things.
I need to hear something.

The pretty chapel comes into view
but the gate is shut —
more of a church than I thought.
I consider trespassing, but for what?
Clearly, saviors don't do after-hours.
A shame. They're missing out,
as we're all having so much fun.
(Does it qualify as 'missing out'
if you're the one who checks out?)

I keep going till I see a cemetery.
Sometimes it's easier to be with the dead
than with the living (by whom, I suppose
I mean I, myself).

I pull off and park, crunch intentionally across the gravel
towards the clusters of headstones.
No stage or deity or fuel pedal to contend with.
Everyone knows that monsters are welcome here.
I move as if I belong.

On three sides, the burial field hugs the edge
of an at-ease forest, serpentine highway on the fourth.
Vehicles whoosh by, leaving some inexplicable
gentleness in their violent wake. The hush

hovering over us is ordinary, which seems
like a mistake.

Instead of wandering,
I am standing still, scanning names
and dates, most in worn script.
A few fresh and clear-cut.

To the left of my nearly-shredded tennis shoe,
lies someone who made it till last month.
Eighty-two. I count from where I am.
I call it too long. I picture a montage of their life —
childhood stings and glories, a mergement into self-
doubt. Inevitable friction with what was supposed to be
safe. The love games, the shimmering sex, the squandered
chances, the yawning years of routine. The soul winters.
Swellings of grief. The surprise radiance of raindrops
clinging to the sharp eaves at dawn. Sparkling beloveds,
whose presence persevered against the worst
of everything. Terrifying devotion, insatiable questing,
angry simmer of aging. All the tender things
that went untold. All the scarring. All the burning.
All the ash. I wonder if they would say
it was worth it.

27 degrees and dropping. I didn't bring a coat.
My threadbare breath steams up into my eyes.
The chill cleaves into me. I wonder
what cold does to bones, how much
rot gets into what is sealed off,

how many cycles of expand-thaw-contract
until fragility defines you. I wonder when I
crossed channels one too many times
and stopped thinking about the dead.

Just like the adrenaline in my veins
the daylight is draining away.
A few more inhales of ice, blinks of flame
are sufficient to recast reality
and force presence.
The monster still has a body.

I turn to scuffle back to the car, and I see
the grave I was looking for.
(There are always one of these.)
Sunburst etched on it. Neat-edged border around it.
Christmas tree next to it.
The stillness hovering around us
is not emptiness.
This one's not waiting for a resurrection.
This one isn't always alone.

Something I can't see breathes on the monster.

There are no answers.
There is just this sacred shrine. There is
a fluorescent orange streak slung low
on the hips of the western sky.
There are horrible, unimaginative fake flowers
on the resting place two plots over, and a battery-powered

lantern that will stay lit tonight.
There are thick, lazy power lines buzzing over my head,
and an ugly, greenish, bass-bumping Ford Explorer
whipping past this place.

There are visible, web-strung things.

They say pain is the great equalizer.
They're wrong. I think
'witness' is the word they're looking for.

I hear unreasonable birdsong,
and the sky's on fire.
Something in my chest untwists.
I'm leaving, not because the monster is at peace,
but because I have locked eyes with her
and she doesn't need to die, she needs to be fed.
I'm leaving because the moon is going to rise, and people
still dream up reasons to love each other,
and the dead deserve another round of warm company
sometime. Because the story of every soul
runs long.

The shadows lose their bruising, just a bit,
while the frost presses close.
I have decided
I will take the long way home.

Poetics

All the places I've left behind
swallowed up any holes that remained
no unfillable gaps
        no empty chair
                no irreplaceability
                        in my wake

Once, someone even told me, *after you were gone*
it was like you never existed

If I could be less honest I'd subtly imply
that I'm a better person
        than those that forget
that I'll choose the blood over the water
that I'll chain myself to the anchor of definitions
        & drop it overboard
that I'll hemorrhage for years
        from the gaping wound created
        by someone exiting the doors of my heart

But I'm not any better
I've abandoned the begetters & taught myself
to scent out the wellsprings
I've learned to carry keys & bolt cutters
I've improved my practice of self-preserving
cauterization, the blunting of the raw edge
with fire & salt

I tell myself
if they can erase you
you were never meant
to leave a mark

I tell myself
I will no longer sacrifice
      the future on the altar of the past
nor martyr the present
      in the name of a potential tomorrow

Nowadays, if you feel no pain when we part
I purge you from my system
like it's my motherfucking job

I tell myself
I will no longer suffer
for poetics

It is a lie
but it is what
I tell myself

Split

In the park with a lake, I lay spine to blades
of grass and hold strands of my hair
up against the light.
A few tendrils branch at the ends,
as if they remember all rifts are origin points,
and they see the value in going splayed, separate ways.

I still have trouble fathoming
how something so finely-spun had the capacity
to split. Like a personality, I struggle to integrate.
I don't care for the villain in me, but I'm told I'm
not allowed to kill her. This is irritating.
Everyone knows you're supposed to get rid of
the bad guy. Even the four-year-olds on the playground
recognize this — they have no use for nuance.
Bad is the opposite of good. People are one or the other.
An enemy inspires solidarity, and a united opposition.

Stretched out in the sun, hovering between shades of blue,
I remember the way the darkness had soft edges
when you told me what a good person I am. I remember
how I rolled my eyes, and told you to run that by your therapist.
'Stubborn modesty is actually self-obsession', mine said, 'which is
an absence of true self.' I ignored her. I know myself well.
I've always preferred to hate me over anyone else beating me
to it. Some people are addicted to painkillers, some to the pain,
all of us to altered states of belief.

I pry clover stems apart beneath a sweetgum, ringed by its
lethal-looking seed pods. A boy once told me the spiky balls
under the tree could shoot you with poisoned blood.
In your pregnant twenties, his metaphor is staggering.
When you're six, it's just terrifying, and you are furious when
an adult informs you of your misconception. Today, the trust
issues are about my willingness to believe, instead of his
willingness to lie.

A breeze creases the surface of the lake and I count
the seconds between crests and troughs. I count the years
between when we were good and when I became bad, as if
gray is not an honest color. I do not want the weight of
subtle distinctions. I just want to be four.
I want to be told that I am acceptable, and that I have time
to become wise, and that I deserve to be angry.
I want someone else to take me home, clean my face
and tell me stories with safe endings.

Another keratin thread from my head has ended
in a small white dot, diverging into halves.
Split hairs result in overall weakness; yet splitting the tab
feels like strength. Keeps my sense of preservation intact
when I suspect the other would prefer me at their mercy.
I am full of fear, and drama. Pink ham torn from the
bone. Split pea soup is a fancy name for using up
the leftovers.

The word 'using' feels bad when discussing people.
But maybe using is all we do. Maybe we're all just
polite trippers, constantly scoring off each other,
bumming companionship, solutions, and proof.
Attachments are fixes, offering warmth, portal, release.
A reason, a mirror, a distraction from the mirror.
Atonement. I don't believe in altruism, though I took
bad acid for a good cause, then sharpied the impact
on a stall door: *I was here.*
I was real, once.

Everyone wants every high to last.
In this vein, I supported my bad habits
with good arguments.

The light is hitting the waves of the lake the way it does
at the height of June, like golden days are eternal.
On the summer solstice after Y2K, a fifteen-year-old
with bipolar disorder accidentally took ten times the usual
dose of LSD. For thirteen, gorgeous years, her life was
no longer partitioned between euphoria and despair.
Sometimes what they call bad is what cures you,
and too much of a thing is good.

Later, she grew up and gave birth. The PPD
did its fracturing work.
Not everything remains as it should.

Genesis is about division, and math isn't hard for me.
I've stopped wanting to be good
medicine for a bad deal.

In the churning water, the gap grows wider
between peak and plunge. I know now
split ends are caused by carelessness, and being
absent from myself does not induce fondness
in my heart. I am undoing an addiction to devotion,
severing your image from my reflection.
For better or worse,
I am not a woman who will swallow
enough of the bad to stay good.

Ten Word Poems

Doomed Romance

Let me
tell you
exactly
how I feel
about us

Favorite Compliment from Therapy

I can see why
religious men
do not like you

*My Mom Would Say I've
"Gone Off the Deep End"*

I'd say
her shallows
aren't as safe
as she pretends

body diptych

i.

the ribs of a child   shine
 through his translucent skin
sanctified starvation
 between the river and the sea

hair is thin ginger sprinkled atop his skull
   teeth   too small
     in a face like a freshly sharpened pencil
bright panic twists his pupils, swarming
  darkness   devours   until this is
             all
               there is

and he's not the only one
not the only one
the only one

and i rage that to wear a body is a curse
and i want to know, how soon can we die?

ii.

    the breast of a lover   glows
    luminous under a full moon
    winter fire, sinner's worship
    against the silk-edged darkness

lips ink-glide across the pages of my senses
        scapula cups   my cheek
fingertips trace this time-stamped treasure map
    stripped-bare surfaces of our shape, a melting
    every border   evanesces   until we're
        all
        there is

    and we're not the only ones
        not the only ones
          the only ones

and i swear that to wear a body is a gift
and i want to know, how long can we live?

What Dreamers Do

He brings a square, gold-colored tupperware
        out to the yard.
Standing before the cinder-frosted logs
at the fringe of the fading bonfire,
        all elementary-school-aplomb,
        he tells me
he is going to 'put smoke inside the box.'

I hold my tongue.
The crickets don't quit their evening tune-up
        as he takes off the lid,
twists and dips the right-angled container into the swirls
        of varying shades of gray.
The sun keeps setting
        in the wake of an equinox
that has split the difference
        between doubt and light.
I have let so many dreams
        pass into mist.

In his palms, the square becomes a diamond
        hovering in the silvery haze.

His cloud-colored t-shirt slopes along growing shoulders
as he practices an innocent defiance of physics.

It's the old story: seeking to capture
        what will always disappear.

I feel an ancient dirge echo in my chest.
Yesterday, a friend sent me a poem
about what it's like
to routinely experience invisibility.
It feels close,
        and I am frightened.

The breeze shifts and blows the acrid vapor
up from the coals into my sight,
but I don't move.
I stay,
watching the wind steal hope.

While tears tease the edges of my eyes,
my dreamer persists.
The dreamers always do.
Like seeds unafraid of the dirt,
they're built to burst apart,
rebirth through rupture.

Close to the waning glow of his experimental hearth,
the patient work continues.
I unlock to the whispers. Within, without.

I feel the coolness of the coming autumn night.
A heat cycle broken.
Sundown sparks waves of wonder
for the fuckery of time.

Tomorrow I will get up and do the tomorrow things —
scrawl the edits and the underlines,

impale my heart on the jagged headlines,
heft the next lucky load of clothing into the dryer.
Chafe through the latest 'opportunity' in my inbox,
savor the taste of a sweet, smooth phrase
under my tongue.
Hold on to any hand that feels like home.

I will try
to refuse to give in
to the treachery of despair,
spawned by living in a world of castles
surrounded by ash heaps.

Tomorrow
I will try
to glimpse the diamond-life
dancing in the smoke.

I watch the last of the fire's sooty breath
        curl into the sky.
The shadows have gone long.

My scientist examines his empty box,
while a whip-poor-will
fills its lungs to bursting.

[   ]

the cornstalks are paper-dry
         and dead

brilliant blue lights
blister the paint jobs of vehicles
it's a harsh beauty
         because it *is* beautiful
but it's costing something

when i look away
         my eyes paint lime-green streaks
         in the sky

it's a friday in november
         and i am hollowed out
every holy sight
         hurts
the only spark i can summon
            comes
                when i think of you
         but you're not here
            anymore

the squirrel leaps
         — at first i think it's a bird
         the angle   into the top of the tree
         is so flight-like —
it almost   loses its grip

but grasps
      with whatever toenails a squirrel has
    slings itself, a long   liquid   line
over the busy asphalt   stays alive

who decides these things?
what magician in whose realm
      chooses
which lively, lusty rodent gets to make the cut
      and which one   just misses?
        it's the question
        slowly eroding my faith
            in faith itself

down the street i wait outside the café
      i'm searching for something
    hot to solve the hunger
            but it's not a puzzle
        it's an equation
      you are the missing numeral
        and no one has an answer key

as i replay the triumph of the furry tree-flier
      trying not to remember the rest
      suddenly the lamps   go out
patrons swivel around, looking for causes
    in the dimming, i realize   effects are more
important   you were so brave, beloved
maybe what matters   isn't an overrated survival
      maybe   it's just the leap itself

The Trade

You are wrecked
Shipless on an island.
Wolfish childling
Tasked to engineer
An armor of pearls
      — Place the sand here
      In this softest lining of your soul.
      No, no, pain means you're doing it right.

Twisting and licking at the incision,
Without memory of beforeness,
Is it any wonder
You do not know to send smoke signals?

When you are eight, the pain is niggling,
But unremarkable.
Curious swollen places,
Puckering all across your form,
Birth little underskin beadings.
After a moon phase, you can see
Pink-specked, opalescent orbs
Pebbling up under your furring flesh.

You are taught, by the tremendous voices
Coming from the ocean,
To consume sand, mouthful by swallow.
      Only this will keep you alive.
      The grist fashions your shield.
      This is your own salvation.

With no one else to ask, you trust this.

As you grow into a pinched ranginess
Amidst jigger fleas and brittle sunburn,
All installed runs beautifully.
Pain becomes thornish.
The irritant never quits.
This frictional sepsis
is a slow, churning burn.
The brooding heat means,
> *You're doing it right.*

The first time you smell hot blood
Spilt on the shore by a preyful bird,
You catch breath at the surge in your jaw.
A quiet quaking in the belly
Startles you.
But the murmurs from the water
Have been clear:
> *To crave is to betray*
> *All hope.*

Years pummel existence.
In the cradle of the night or the womb of the morning,
Punchy red bloomings beneath your skin
Remind you of absence
And void.
Tender lumps shingle the frame of you.
The leanness of your limbs sings
A grating note against the lullabies of the undertow.

In your perennial pacing of the shoreline,
Rounding its edges, clocking the position of the light,
You make a discovery:
The island is shrinking.

All the feathered things are fleeing.
The driftwood is disappearing, stain on the sands
Climbing higher.
Sunscorch presses heavy
On your studded shoulders,
While the emptiness of your innards
Seethes like the incoming tide.

Sleep dwindles, vortexual time sharpens.
Last night your eternal soreness
Drew howls from your throat.

Today, by the rising saltwater,
Gut pulsing,
You are remembering
Every silicic choke,
How each gulp ground out your voice.
You cannot take another grain.

Something has cracked
Through your gumline.
Running tongue along the sharpness,
The ache under your mottled hide
Hurtles to a searing pitch.
A lust to slice

Buzzes in your ribs like a bee swarm,
While the want in your center
Heaves jagged like the surf against a reef.

You kneel and tooth
A blistering crest of your own surface.
Feeling your way by the light of living nightmare
You pierce the throbbing knurl.
This clean pain — fervid relief.

Single stone falls to the wet beach.
It is unbeautiful and gray.
A scarlet drop from your body
Slips from the open wound.

The bright sour of bloodscent
Kindles every sleeping coal in your cells.
What kind of life is worth saving?

The furious waves are roaring,
Ascending at your back.

The sun is going down
In flames.
Something hungry just woke up.

You must eat
And the only thing left
On the island
Is you.

Strawberry Fields

I drove us toward the strawberry fields.
The gray lake looked smaller as I passed it
and the memories grew thicker,
like a swarm of summer winged things
hazing my forward progress.
I asked myself, what, really,
does it take to heal?

Arms of trees reached across the highway
as if they could sense the soreness of my heart
and longed to soothe it.
Chiron is making angles, they tell me,
and that means something?
The road stretches on.
We keep going.

Later, we sit on a wooden bench, rich
in buckets of ruby berries, savoring
the sweetness of tourist-tradition ice cream,
drunk on sunbeams and breezes
of spring. And I think, maybe it's enough
to simply not bleed for a bit.

Guardian

There's an angel posted at the door
of my memories of you.

She doesn't prevent me from entering
but every time I emerge, cursing or crying

or bleeding, or quiet
yet again

she takes the threads I thrust at her
and simply, silently nods.

I wonder sometimes
why she has no reprimands for me.

Maybe this sentry understands
I'm getting free in there.

Maybe this angel once decided
her love doesn't depend on strings, either.

**My friend says a sea anemone
closes up when touched**
for Superbloom

When I was twenty-three & working in a daycare, the fathers of children would touch whatever of mine they felt entitled to. My curving shoulder. Perhaps a flickering elbow. One time, my daringly exposed face. I surged & twisted, & I snarled & did not smile. My boss shrugged, *It doesn't mean anything.* My co-worker scoffed, *It was a joke, why didn't you laugh it off?* My boss & my co-worker said nothing to the fathers.

The video of the shimmering sea anemone presents her assault: ugly, meaty fingers, swiping & frisking. In the wake of the grope, her response is a slow shiver & retreat. A folding in on her own sensitive core. Another frame, more of the same. Gleeful probe. Vanishment. The clip is called "Resilience." In the comments they're begging the hand, *Please — don't.*

When I was twenty-five & in love, the wife of a pastor told me that husbands touch you at the rhythm of their own whims, not yours. She said to expect this, & to comply. I twitched & flared, & I swallowed & did not smile. My mouth asked, *Do we matter?* The wife said, *Just don't fight.* My mouth & the wife said nothing to anyone.

Sea anemones are named after star-laced, land-dwelling blossoms. These bright, young daughters of the wind were born of nectar & the blood of Aphrodite's dead lover. The Mona Lisa species has brilliant carmine-pink petals, & a wide-eyed, welcoming center. One of her selling features: *low-maintenance*. Perfect for display. Able to subsist on just drops of dew & the light of winter.

When I was twenty-six & blooming, a preacher of the gospel touched me like I am something you can own. I did not fight. I thought this was how you absorb oxygen for breathing under-water. I stilled & wilted, & I was quiet & did not smile. My mind demanded, *Why are we drowning?* My furious body spoke only through color. The preacher said nothing to me.

Anemones cannot run, but they can unroot themselves from inhospitable rocks, & they can sting. The most dangerous dwell in the deep currents, far from the coastline. These anemones learned survival. They understood that to stay close to the shore is to put up with rapacious pawing & vicious poaching. Distance equals safety. Except we all know predators will cross the ocean to plant a colony in you.

When I was this-week-old & foolishly kind, a man who pretended we are friends yanked me in close while shaking my hand, & did not let go until he had spewed all his vile, boring whispers into my ear. But I have become a "difficult" woman. I snapped his wrist & shattered glass against his skull, & I laughed at him & then I smiled. Nothing in me had any questions to ask. He had no more "compliments" to deliver. I'm saying something to everyone.

The private lore of the sea anemone is written in redemptive poison. Self-insertion of any shrimpish, tide-pool terrorist into where he doesn't belong activates the venom. She is tentacle & shapeshifter, & legend & lethality. Unlike a jellyfish, she does one better than a Medusa "phase." The prey has become the paralyzer. He'll *wish* he was stone.

When I've been every age & like a scarlet sunrise, the sharks of all the seas have circled. I was expected to stay silent & shrink. But I have simmered & foamed, & I have grown angry & grown teeth. Any contracting posture mistaken for my flinch was just the first bite. My lips ask, *What do we do with the uninvited?* My slit says, *On the first thrust, we eat them alive.* & they, spineless, pathetic pricks, will die screaming.

Curon

Lone ice carver spins
Across the frozen skin
Of a lake of lost memories

Single spire slices
Through the surface
Headstone
Of the vanished village

This turret is a testament
To collective sacrifice —
Dwelling place drowned
By power for power

This has always been the way of it
Not the end
But the way

And still the skater swirls

Darling, let's do the same
Let's burn the sound of our blades
Over what they have stolen
Let's etch vision into ice-bound tides
Let's dance
Across the tombs
Of our swallowed-up cities

Let's live
Like the bells ring on
As if home
Will always be
Ours

i thought it'd feel different

i'm headed north   up the highway
     the dash clock hints   at the darkside of eleven
i catch   the backlit silhouettes   of two bodies
     wending through a motel parking lot
   for a moment   in my mind
        i'm walking with them   tired inn
boasts sallow lamps, blue letters   oncoming dew
     broods in the air   engines   power up
this sparsely-traveled route   i sense the approach
      the presence   the f a d e
   like hope   erasing itself

     a deer crushes through the leaf litter
in the dark   out here   i can hear everything
    except voices

back in my body, i'm still   headed north
    & the song on the speakers   sings
something   about promises
    i can feel all the shards of it   stuck in
along my spine   sharp edges of 'never'   & 'yes'
    & 'will'   some body   always pays
      for pledges

i remember this part   of the road
    a curved rib   -bon out in the country
i think about the day i noticed a hole

                punched through   a generous, inky-edged cloud
wondered what it would be like   to just
        overshoot the turn   a little
    soar   straight through silver   guardrails
up & up   for a moment, towards the circle
i remember how much not-fear i felt   that curious
        liminal peace
               i miss that feeling

slate airspace   on the opposite
            side   of the four-lane
shifted my attention   a storm   sweeping in
        windpress & water rinse
        transference of the weight
      carried   across miles
a thought   *maybe*   *stay for that*

i blink   against high beams in the rearview
      i'm headed north   & i thought it'd feel
different   like   i'm about to find
what we're all   always chasing
        but i don't

i remember this road   histories haze like
      mosquitoes at sundown   multiple lives
replicating & reducing & reshaping   within the living
      drives   when "chocolate" by the 1975
was the only sound   that kept me   believing in
tomorrow   drives into the wrung-out familiar, turnoffs & dead
    -ends measuring up   to their names

i remember this road   drives past the known
    to the lesser-known   a few days' escape, a varnish
of respite   slicked over the ennui   i am nothing &
    i am everyone & i am   a prisoner in solitary
with a   perfect   bay window view

i'm headed north   & i recall the night   years too late
    after chasing the sunset   i sent you the song
unzipped my soul, let the dark   out   to play
    told the whole & momentary truth

 you replied   you tried   so hard   to make
me heal   it didn't work   i healed, but
  not the way you wanted
    you're disappointed in me   so am i

i'm headed   north
    i thought i'd see   the stars this far out of town
but there's a thick, wet film   clogging up the skyscape
    it figures, 'cause   you can't ever reach
    what you can see   anyway

i'm headed north   once, i pictured   a ledge
    something to accidentally   slip off of
not because i want   to die   but
    because i am   weary
of enduring   living
    i'm not picturing that now

i'm headed north   i don't know   where i'm going
    i'm just
          on my way

i thought it'd feel different than this   but it doesn't
    it's   quieter   & noisier at the same time
the soundtrack is wrong   the mood's a drag
     & the miles pass slow   i'm still lonely

i thought   it'd feel different   than   this
    like i was   not only   on the brink
of getting what i always wanted   but like i knew
        what that was, too

i thought it'd feel   different   than this
    i remember how   it used to feel
it's not the same   i can't say   anything
    has improved
       but it's not the same   as it was
  that's something   anyway
      i remember what it   cost
   to come   this far
    that's not nothing

i thought   it'd feel different   than   this
   like, good   like, better   like i was the heroine
like someone else   besides me   was choosing
    to believe
       it's   just me

i remember this road　　　i'm headed north　　i thought
　　　it'd feel　　　different　　　　　　　than this
　　　　　　　　　　　　it doesn't
　　　but i am still
　　　　　　　　　　headed north

The Thing with Fangs
after Emily Dickinson

"Hope" is the thing with fangs
That prowls in the soul
And chafes against the ancient chains -
She's scenting what fear stole

And time is not a tamer
No feast has ever filled
It's not for want of trying
But Hope they've never killed

I've heard her howling late at night -
There're rumors she got free -
In league with Love - and forging keys -
She dwells in possibility

Venus Retrograde

On the full supermoon in August,
while the goddess planet goes reverse,
I wait.

Next to my blanket of woven threads,
even the veined grass
is humming. Tree crickets
sing this night alive, electric.

I'm supposed to starwatch tonight.

I couldn't tell you why or how I know this —
the buzzing under my skin, the sharp
taste in the water, or something
about the surprise of my own reflection
in the mirror.
I do not understand,
but I've come to the field anyway.
The whole world is prickling in anticipation.

Luna tips up past the treeline,
all silver-golden glory.
Ripened abundance.
This is the moment the dark and I
have been straining for,
        and we exhale.

Peace of the devotee settles
through bone and sinew.
The present is wide and the universe
is generous. I lean back

And see
a long, bright line of glowing green dots,
spaced   perfectly   apart,
streaking across the sky.
Wild, neon not-geese.

Shock-stung, I try to count.
Six, seven, nine…

My psyche staggers, brain bending
with questions that don't quit,
about origamied dimensions and interstellar ships,
about the story of what a friend's sister saw once,
flickering in the desert
against the blurred vastness of the spacescape.

Ten silent orbs glide with precision,
disappear right above the moon.
I've never been this breathless.

For a few pounding minutes
I believe in a riven veil.
My harassed skeptic
hushes.

Then I google.

My beautiful cosmic query
        is answered:
they were only
Elon's starlink satellites.

Certainty is a wounded hound
howling. I am an empty room
with cold corners.

Maybe every beautiful thing is a false prophet.

A summer breeze moves on.
I am the miserable insect stuck
on a web I misread as road.
All the magic is trick and
I weep.

h/ex

the night i dreamed of your force on my body
    your seeking heat and unsummoned hands
    my crystal voice shattering under your deafness
i woke and walked out of the house
screamed rage, pure and acid, into the atmosphere

immediately, lightning answered me
ripped edges blazing in the sky

careful, you.

the elements know my name
i did not hesitate
to give them yours

Canyon

I thought the sharpness of early spring had burnt off,
but I crossed the threshold
& my bare arms birthed chill bumps.

Funny thing, a woman's body — all the electric
knowings of the prey animal, every nerve ending a doubt mark
between desire & desire.

At the gym, a man, on whose progressive feelings
I am meant to perform emotional taxidermy,
peacocks his alleged disgust for the systemic sexism
embellishing a business email.

How did you push back on that when you replied? I ask.
Surprise, we do not go for coffee.

When I was seventeen & sleepless, I visited the south rim
of the Colorado River Gorge. The paint-like streaks across the rocks
dizzied me, & I saw that beauty existed loudest
in the distance between two points.

How can anything be gorgeous under a microscope?
In missionary I still dream of walking on the ceiling.

A century ago, Mary E. J. Colter, architect & designer
for the Fred Harvey Company (hirer of "pretty" waitresses),
bridged worlds by weaving wonder with what already belonged.
People liked the way her way-stops on the rail lines told stories.

Here is an old tale: a woman touches everything
& makes it more.
Somewhere, a man profits.

I am good at making nothing out of everything. My stories
demand killed darlings. No one had to teach me yearning,
which is the only language that fails to communicate.

At the equinox, a red fox darts through the shin-tangle, & I call it
a sign, because the light-gap is narrow & I am a lonely optimist.

What if what you want doesn't exist? the therapist
asks with obscene gentleness.

Colter faced stone & etched her will into it, breathing out smoke
with style. Meanwhile, synthetic carpet can still leave ridge marks
in my knees. I choked on my own appetite.

There is desert between my thighs & lava in my throat.
I've never been so unable
to arch my back
across any more fault lines.

Bottom of the Wheel

I.

A rare snow has glazed the morning,
stilling down the dispassionate pulse of the ordinary.
Cropped winter fields, fence frames, stiff pine trees,
refashioned into illusion. Perfect for postcards.

The crunch underfoot has blunted.
Red mud scratches back to the surface.
I turn and walk home ahead of the stragglers.
Stark descent vibrates in my chest, like we had

pierced briefly through an ocean to clear air, but now
drug beneath the surface, breathing is hard again.
With every step, I feel the edges darken. Familiar
blanket falling across my body, same color as

the ash-gray sky. Endlessness of unbent
road   under   half-lit sun   this is all   this is
all there is   unquantifiable   void   holding
you between its paws   panting   hungry

II.

it is too quiet in my screaming head

III.

I reach the mailbox, robotically check its craw.
Pull out last week's junk paper
so I can carry it indoors, drop it in the trash —
I am such a loser I don't even recycle.

Out slides a seed catalog.
Plum-purple blossoms cascade across the cover,
wreathed by impossibly glossy, green leaves.
Neon sign blazing in the midst of the flat obedient.

The cliché is unbearable, but it works.

On cue, a voice laughs in the distance.
Emily sings in my ear. Somewhere,
a car door bangs, cheerful and present.

The light is washed pale, and my toes
are going numb through the bottoms of these boots,
but I remain,
an unstiffening statue. *Breathe in.*
Breathe out.

IV.

Sometimes you don't send enough of the love
letters that you write, yet
you get one back
anyway.

Dear Forgetful,
Of course there is more.
But it's winter, you darling fuckface.
The wheel turns. More is
just not here
yet.

Strange, Small Town

Twilight hums blue. I go alone for a walk in a strange, small
town. I feel the dog's black bark before I ever hear it. At the
stoplight, everyone has somewhere to be. I do not. But I
pretend I am on my way, defiant fist in my blocked throat,
your vampiric trace ever-present. I home for the lonely woods
and unfamiliar backroads. No one knows who I am or who
I envy. I've learned risk takes the edge off of need and I am
too needy to avoid the edge. I'm too everything, too harsh, too

uptight, too aware of the knotted stitch on the back of your
elbow, too late to catch the sunset glitter. A dry limb snaps.
I try to go blank, but you, you have returned, you and the burn
of those two nights with your grip around my neck. All beautiful
unattainability and heartless heat. I'd kill for more. I hate myself
for how easy it is to get hungry again. Around an empty bend,
hemmed in by tall trees still early-spring naked, a pickup vibrates
past. Slowly. A minute later my shoulders are still tensed, like my
thighs as you strobed between them. I pass a dense hollow,

feel the cold of somewhere the sun doesn't hit. All the dead leaves
remind me of the body they drug from the forest two years ago
in November. I hate November. No, that's a lie, I love November, I'm
just starving. Everything is turning static in the halflight. Thinking
in absolutes makes me feel powerful, impossible. Everywhere is
deviant and fascinating when you don't belong. I'm right off time.
My maps app doesn't know where I am, but I do: just where I can't
find an answer, exactly how I like it. Nothing changes. I'm still here
without you, curling at the edges, holding my breath for never.

seventeen

ragged bass throbs in our cores. we raft
on rings of neon light across a youthful sea

seeking the fringe of the cramped floor. we're
older than most & we know it & don't care.

still moving with the electric waves
of sound, the woman i sort of know grabs

a cheap plastic cup. *doesn't it remind you,* she
shouts with a grin, *of when you were seventeen?*

i sling backwards in time to weekends
wiping baseboards in my mother's house,

music from the wrong century humming
through my headphones.

the light does not shift. invariability
is one of the discovered virtues.

there are so many more deadly sins than seven.
i blink against the whitewater of memories.

my mind loops evenings spent in a hollow
sanctuary of a room, writing down

dreams i'd later light with matches.
i remember listening to fireworks

beyond the glass, watching peer-aged strangers
on the street flaunt bare knees, strut like my life

was a scam & repentance a myth. hot spit
of the preacher down my neck, distress rash

spidering across my sternum. i visited
a mall like a museum — voyeuristic

everything untouchable. apocalypse-printed
brain, hymn-hazed hunger.

devotion begs for sacrifice, & i coaxed
quiet the restlessness roaming narrow veins,

salivating ache. i fed her scritta paper. i drowned
her in silence. i filed her fangs flat.

i let her out in the nightmares. i buried her
behind the baby blanket in the closet.

i worshipped stories of tombs
till i became one.

i shake my head & laugh a little. *i've never been
seventeen*, i answer. a dark spark flickers

through the features of my friend, joy lines
dissolving around her eyes. her drink clips

against the table as she stares out into the pulsing
crowd. *me neither.* scar believes burn. i know

nothing except we are kin, & we are both
grateful tonight does not remind us of then.

i wonder how many of us has ever had
what we've imagined seventeen gives you.

i wonder if it matters, if i was cheated
or saved. like fresh air, the room floods

back into my body. the dj drops a track
& everybody else begins to sing. i do not

know the words, but a knot of dancers
cheers infectiously. this beat is beautiful

& now is now. i choose to revel. i am here,
& i've never been this young before.

Not Cold Anymore

When your lips lit mine
On some street I've never found the name of
You struck us a suspension of time

All that mattered was the moment —
Tangled strings of the past
Phantom futures
Didn't exist

We hung halfway between the realms
All wet press and tilt
Roaming seams separating skin
Soft thumb sliding through shadowlands
Testing the thin edge of honesty

You breathed me like you knew me
Like you new how to shape a pulse
Make it into music
Like you understood how to interpret
The echoes shuddering back from the void
After the dance ends

You felt me
Like everything is real
And fleeting
      and sacred
           and matters

Heartbeat by inhale
You robbed me of my stiff-necked cynicism

Is this what it's like to be fearless?

A streetlight glowed on the chest of midnight
Maybe not every burning thing leaves scars

Later in the deep blue of the dark
I could believe
Winter had only ever been a dream
That every frozen thing can thaw

I could still see a ring of angelfire
Kindling around the moon

The Tender Untethered

You lope along the wet gravel road,
all patient budding and goaty bliss.
Your three-foot frame glows against the fresh face of the world,
while your muddy shoes kick up the understory.

Yesterday you pressed your bare sole against mine.
We measured up past my arch.
I am supposed to be afraid; but time is only earth-magick,
the unfurling of a new familiar,
a sense of being found
somewhere within a circle that's still spinning.
I release the doubts, let them float away like feathers.

A truck rumbles past, slows and stops.
The driver lies to my face.
Nothing we remember is exactly true.
Our plucky gray matter fills in the gaps with hard-won montages
of shiny stories, craven fears, and colored energies.

There was a kid in the pickup, too.
Years compress under memory, layers squashing together
like the soaked clay we stand on.
I remember passengership.
Since I won't be afraid,
I feel longing on their behalf.
I whisper sorrow for the way
 a wheel cycles.

The tire tracks walk us home.
You keep on
climbing towards the crest of the hill,
vital with wonder.

Lacings of light have torn
through the slate of the postpartum sky.
The neon green poplars radiate some kind of truth.
I fix my eyes on you, the tender untethered.

I know like I know my own names,
heaven is a backlit myth
and the angels already walk among us.
Nothing bad should happen to anyone
and a breath
holds the fragile world together,
like a promise
balanced on the fulcrum of belief —
at any moment we could plunge.

I choose to root myself here:
that even this
is good.

Notes

"Book of Judges" references the books of Ezra and Judges in the Jewish Nevi'im (Tanakh) and the Christian Old Testament. In Ezra 10, the Israelites attempt ethnic purification via mass divorce. In Judges 4, Jael invites the captain of an enemy army into her tent, lulls him to sleep, then drives a tent peg through his skull, effectively winning a war.

"When the Sun Goes Down in Winter" is an ekphrastic poem in response to the oil painting *Frozen Streets* by Maine artist Colin Page.

Scull Shoals was a paper mill community in Greene County, Georgia, built on lands belonging to the Creek Nation. The place was likely named after skeletal remains found in prehistoric earthworks near the Oconee River. Several brutal encounters took place between intruders and natives throughout its early colonization.
Flooding destroyed sections of the community in both 1841 and 1887, due to unsustainable forms of agriculture. Poor farming techniques, especially cotton farming that utilized the forced labor of enslaved Black people, eroded so much soil that the river rapids which powered the mill are buried beneath an estimated fourteen feet of silt.

"The Spiritual Discipline of Seeing" is based on the final lines of Wendell Berry's "Sabbaths—1979, IV." The golden shovel form was created by Terrance Hayes, who published a poem by the same title in 2010. Hayes ended each line of his poem with the successive words from Gwendolyn Brooks' "We Real Cool."

"Imagine if Jephthah's daughter..." references Judges 11 in the Jewish Nevi'im (Tanakh) and the Christian Old Testament, as well as many other biblical passages. Jephthah, a warrior, promises to sacrifice by fire whatever comes out the door of his home to greet him after battle, if God will afford him a victory. Jephthah defeats the opposing army. The first being out to meet him upon his return home is his only child, a daughter.

This poem also uses the phrase "red tent," an archetype of nurturing communities for women, arising from Anita Diamant's novel of the same title. The novel references a rabbinical Jewish practice of segregating menstruating women from broader society.

Finally, the last line of "Imagine if Jephthah's daughter..." is now considered a mainstream compliment; like many beautiful bits of language the internet has popularized, the phrase has its roots in queer subculture, specifically Black and Latino drag ball tradition.

"Monster" contains a line about the "long story of our souls," directly gathered from author Perdita Finn.

"Split" references the story of an LSD study subject, known only as "AV," as related in the article "LSD Overdoses: Three Case Reports," by Mark Haden and Birgitta Woods, published January 2020.

"Curon" was directly inspired by a video of Swiss figure skater and travel blogger Michaela Carrot blading around a half-submerged bell tower on the surface of Lake Resia (Reschensee, Lago di Resia) in South Tyrol, Italy. The village that once housed the tower's chapel, Curon, was covered over by an artificial lake in 1950, despite the dissent of the local residents. The fourteenth century spire is all that remains above the waters. Though they were removed seventy-five years ago, some say you can still hear bells ringing from the tower in the winter.

"The Thing with Fangs" is after Emily Dickinson's extraordinary " 'Hope' is the thing with feathers."

"Canyon" references Mary Elizabeth Jane Colter, a Minnesotan who spent decades in the Southwest as an architect and designer for the Santa Fe Railroad and the Fred Harvey Company. She engineered inns and hotels and state park structures that highlighted, instead of erased, the styles found in Indigenous American culture. Several of her buildings are still intact in Grand Canyon National Park. She considered the La Posada Hotel in Winslow, Arizona to be her masterwork.

Content Advisement

Instances of grief, death, consensual sex, offensive language, and substance use are not included in this list.

Religious trauma and spiritual abuse (defined as manipulation, oppression, isolation, and control within religious settings and systems, through the weaponization of power, shame, and fear)

"Book of Judges" – references to biblical narratives, spiritual abuse *(throughout)*

"Imagine if Jephthah's daughter…" – references to biblical passages/phrases/narratives *(throughout)*

"The Trade" – spiritual abuse *(extended metaphor)*

"seventeen" – spiritual abuse *(throughout)*

Violence

"Book of Judges" – references to instances of biblical violence *(multiple, brief)*

"Mosaic" – school shooting *(extended metaphor)*

"Imagine if Jephthah's daughter…" – references to instances of biblical violence *(brief)*, mild violent imagery *(throughout)*

"Hitman" – mild violent imagery *(brief)*

"body diptych" – references the forced starvation and genocide of the Palestinian people in Gaza *(first half)*

"My friend says a sea anemone closes up when touched" – violent imagery *(multiple, brief)*

Sexual violence and assault

"Book of Judges" – reference to a violent rape *(brief)*

"Imagine if Jephthah's daughter…" – reference to biblical rape laws *(brief)*

"My friend says a sea anemone closes up when touched" – sexual assault *(extended metaphor)*

"h/ex" – sexual assault *(brief)*

Mental health

"The Trade" – self-harm *(brief)*

"Monster" – suicidal thoughts *(throughout)*

"Split" – reference to self-hatred, suicide (*brief*)

"i thought it'd feel different" – suicidal thoughts *(throughout)*

"Bottom of the Wheel" – depression *(first half)*

"Strange, Small Town" – self-hatred *(brief)*

Acknowledgments

I am wildly grateful to my myriad creative communities, including Tattered Writers; Athens Word of Mouth; Beats, Rhymes, and Life; Wild Soul; Superbloom Society; Cara, Emma, and Michelle; and my line dance crew. You consistently make me believe in art, in togetherness, in myself, in humanity, in joy.

To Lauren Wilde, who helped me cast, track, and remain in trust with this project, and was a voice of belief when I doubted, my sincere appreciation. To the muse.

Deepest thanks to the first readers of this completed project, Patty Tacuri (your support and stories are endlessly inspiring to me — grateful to share community with you), Deepika Gomes (the magic, beauty, and perspective you bring to the world, friend, is not to be underestimated), J.R. Barner (your thoughtful read, plus the reams of quality poetry you've introduced me to, have both been invaluable), and Sarah Spradlin (you may be the most generous soul I've ever met, dear heart — for the time, the questions, the eyes, the tenderness, thank you). I knew if I could send it to you all, I could send it anywhere.

The Group That Shall Not Be Named. We're five years deep, beautifuls, and just *look at us go*. You all are the real real. Growing beside you is an honor.

To my darlings, Stephanie, Ellie, Molly, Anna. Knowing you has at times saved my very soul. Thank you for choosing to be your full selves, for forever becoming, for believing in me, and for not just listening to me, but *hearing* me. I adore you.

To my kiddos. I will never be disappointed in who you are. I am for you.

Amanda Dzimianski

is a lifelong writer, practicing poet, and the author of *Ache is a Passport: Love Letters to Survivors of Spiritual Abuse*. She grew up in the IFB cult and chooses to be neither a shiny, happy person, nor a virtuous woman. Her traditional education has been minimal, her submission history is abysmal, and both are the least interesting things about her. She is a strengths-based and self-publishing coach, and a story alchemist. She lives near Athens, Georgia.

Scan the code to connect to more of Amanda's work.

www.ingramcontent.com/pod-product-compliance
Lightning Source LLC
Chambersburg PA
CBHW070644030426
42337CB00020B/4159